# The Comic Legend of

# William McGonagall

**Created by**
**Charles Nasmyth**

A pictorial story based on the life of
**The World's Worst Poet**
*with illustrated verse*

WAVERLEY
BOOKS

# Acknowledgements

I am indebted to Richard Demarco without whose encouragement I may never have completed the pictures for this book. Also, I am very grateful for the support shown me by numerous other friends and colleagues, but special thanks go to: David Mabbs of the Rockcliffe Gallery, Stanley Mazur and his colleagues at Celtic Arrow Media, David Kett of Dundee City Library; Michael Crichton, Andy Naismith, Andy McDougall, Terry Ann Newman, Calum MacDonald and Chris Pearson. Last but not least, my gratitude also goes to my wife, Mary, for her endless patience and down-to-earth common sense.

To this, I should add posthumous thanks and apologies to the following artists for the inspiration they have provided – with varying degrees of subtlety – for some of the images that appear in this book: John Everett Millais, William Holman Hunt, Henry Wallis, Alexander Nasmyth, Caspar David Friedrich, Peter Paul Rubens, Michelangelo Buonarotti and Edouard Manet.

Published 2007 by Waverley Books Ltd,
David Dale House, New Lanark, ML11 9 DJ, Scotland

ISBN 978 1 902407 53 1

Printed and bound in Poland by OZGraf S.A.

# Foreword

I was delighted when Ron Grosset, the publisher, approached me to write a foreword to Charles Nasmyth's extraordinary graphic novel, *The Comic Legend of William McGonagall*, because I have watched it evolve over a period of two years. The first time I saw the then incomplete artwork was in April 2005, when Charles invited me along to Stewart's Melville College and asked my advice on how to bring the work to a wider public. I loved what I saw and knew it should eventually become a book, but also realized that such an unusual work would need a little more exposure before it was offered up to the scrutiny of publishers.

I introduced Charles to Andy McDougall and Andy Naismith, my two friends who run the Edinburgh Art Fair, and they gave the work a very successful public airing at the Corn Exchange in November 2005. Further support came from David Mabbs of the Rockcliffe Gallery and Stanley Mazur of Celtic Arrow Media, who arranged to film a conversation that I had with Charles about an exhibition of the *Comic Legend* at the Baron's Craig Hotel. This resulted in a DVD that proved a useful tool of persuasion for David Kett, another McGonagall enthusiast, to mount an exhibition of the completed work at Dundee City Library's Wighton Centre in the spring of 2007. The opening of this exhibition attracted the attention of radio and television news as well as the press. During the course of the exhibition, Ron Grosset, who had recently published Cam Kennedy and Alan Grant's very successful graphic novel, *Kidnapped*, paid a visit. The rest is history.

Every time readers look at the pictures in this book, they will see something new and something different to make them laugh. This has been my experience each time I look at them afresh. You will also keep discovering images of celebrities, politicians, artists and writers. You will find cryptic references to the events and failings of our own world. This is because Charles Nasmyth has taken us on a journey – and it is my belief that all meaningful artistic endeavours are a journey – through the life of William McGonagall. What his life stood for is so much more important than the doggerel which he misguidedly believed to be poetry. This work seems to say that McGonagall may have been delusional, but he is also one of us. In this way Nasmyth continually tests our humanity.

One image I find myself coming back to is the one that illustrates McGonagall's journey to Balmoral in an attempt to read his poems to Queen Victoria. The poet is posed on an outcrop of rocks in exactly the same manner as Caspar David Friedrich's *Wanderer above the Sea of Mist*. The spires of Balmoral and the shape of Lochnagar pierce an ocean of cloud, but all of this is turned into something terrifying. Floating above the idyllic scene, Nasmyth shows Queen Victoria in a kind of horse-drawn chariot that is transforming into a snarling dog. It is based on McGonagall's own description of a nightmare he had the night before he arrived at the castle. I look at this astonishing picture and think what a wonderful animated film this would make!

Time and time again, in the very beautiful pages of this book, we find McGonagall's dreams and his hopes of glory thwarted by harsh reality. Then there is the delightfully farcical picture of him taking the title role in a production of *Macbeth* and causing a riot because he refuses to succumb to Macduff's sword in the final scene. Even when this poor devil had an advantage, he only ever succeeded in transforming it into a negative. I also love the surreal imagery of the poetry illustrations and particularly the one of 'The Tay Bridge Disaster' that shows McGonagall in bed with Marilyn Monroe smoking a cigarette; then, after a few moments, you realize the bed head is a tombstone.

This is an important work because although Robert Burns has to be Scotland's most popular poet, I am sure that William McGonagall would come in a close second – even if for wholly different reasons. I really can't call these pictures illustrations. They are serious works of art. What Charles Nasmyth has done here is to add a new and much needed twist to the tale of a poor, simple, badly treated and misguided soul. *The Comic Legend of William McGonagall* uses the poet's trials and tribulations to show us that we are all teetering on the brink of catastrophe; peering over the edge of the abyss. McGonagall comes across as brave and bold, with all the sure footedness of a great artist, and Nasmyth treats him with great compassion. But, strangely enough, when I hear his doggerel or think of his life, he never fails to make me laugh – and so does this book!

Professor Richard Demarco CBE

# The Artist's Notes

This work was the product of two midlife crises – mine and McGonagall's. A midlife crisis is that point when you realize you have wasted the first half of your life, and it is now time to decide how you are going to waste the other half. For McGonagall, sometimes known as 'the Clown Prince of Poets', the decision was easy. Having wasted the first half of his life as a penniless weaver, he decided he would spend the second half as a penniless poet. Besides, he was acting on the direct orders of the Muse who had visited him during the Dundee holiday week and whispered her instructions in his ear.

Unfortunately, the Muse did not present herself to me in quite such a dramatic fashion. Unlike McGonagall, I did not decide to forsake my day job, as a teacher, in pursuit of artistic glory, but just changed the way I disposed of my spare time. Hitherto this had consisted of painting landscapes. A noble pursuit but one I felt that had not provided enough challenges, even though I still enjoy doing it when I get the chance. No, I wanted to do something different. Naturally, I considered cutting a Highland cow in half and pickling it in formaldehyde, but I didn't know Charles Saatchi – so there wasn't a lot of point. I needed something less messy but more shocking.

My moment of inspiration came at a McGonagall Night Supper, a superbly anarchic event for which the high point of the evening was a recitation of the bard's tragic masterpiece 'The Tay Bridge Disaster'. To give dramatic emphasis to salient points in the verse, a variety of props were required. These ranged from an inflatable sex toy to a toilet bowl filled with dry ice. As the only artist among the performers, I was asked to create some cardboard cut-outs to enlarge the number of props. One was to be of **God** and another of a **catastrophe**. God was easy enough but a catastrophe proved more difficult, until a friend, Richard Alexander, deliberately mispronounced the word **cat-arse-trophy** during a rehearsal. In no time at all I had cut out the shape of a cat perched on top of a trophy, whilst exposing its rear end. It was a satisfyingly surreal image which gave me the idea for a book illustrating the life and poems of the great man. However, I needed to know more.

I had known for many a long year that McGonagall's doggerel had become a byword for all that was bad in poetry, but I hadn't realized that he only decided to abandon his trade as weaver and follow the Muse's command in middle age. I didn't know that he was well versed in the works of Shakespeare and had even tried his hand at acting. I knew nothing of his ill-fated trips to London, New York, Fife and Balmoral.

Most of this information I gleaned from his three published 'autobiographies', all of which contain slightly varied accounts of his adventures. But then there was MacDiarmid's essay, 'The Great McGonagall', which casts some doubt on the authenticity of these stories, claiming that many of them may have been made up by bullies who tormented him. There were I also discovered, when browsing the Internet, those who claimed that McGonagall knew his poetry was bad and only feigned that he was serious to gain public acclaim.

Disentangling fact from fiction was going to be well-nigh impossible; the only thing anyone could be certain of was his desire to be recognized in the face of ridicule, poverty and misfortune. If some of the more bizarre episodes in his 'autobiographies' were made up by others, McGonagall made no attempt to deny them. Even if it had dawned on him that his poetry was bad, he seemed to conduct his life according to the principle that it is better to be known for being awful than not at all.

To my mind though, it is much more likely that he regarded those who ridiculed him as ignorant philistines who simply failed to comprehend his true genius. He was as near as you can get to a nineteenth-century wannabe who missed out on appearing in *Big Brother*, but with the vital difference that he wanted to be famous for following a noble calling – that of poet and tragedian.

Later, in the twentieth century, another individual of doubtful talent, Marilyn Monroe, set out her stall to be recognized as a great actress. She, like McGonagall, certainly achieved fame for reasons other than her ability, and part of that fame, like his, was established by people who abused her and took advantage of her naivety. Bearing this in mind, the reader may be a little less surprised to find Marilyn's glamorous image offset with McGonagall's somewhat shabbier persona on a number of occasions in this book. They may seem an unlikely couple, but they were kindred spirits.

Through stubborn determination, McGonagall created his own comic legend. He seemed to be aware of the myth of the Romantic artist who was prepared to suffer for his individuality and art. His walk from Dundee to Balmoral, in a failed attempt to read his poems to Queen Victoria, is a classic example of this. The trek through the misty mountains to Deeside was a journey that Byron would have understood. After all, the latter had spent some of his youth near Ballater and wrote that well-known and nostalgic piece of verse, 'Dark Lochnagar', in response to his experiences of wild nature. The poem has been much maligned by Byron's own admirers, who feel that the appeal it made to popular sentiment diminishes its value when read alongside his more serious verse. But by comparison with McGonagall's efforts, it sounds positively sublime:

Away ye gay landscapes, ye gardens of roses
In you let the minions of luxury rove
Restore me the rocks where the snowflake reposes
If still they are sacred to freedom and love.
Yet Caledonia, dear are thy mountains
Round their white summits tho' elements war
Tho' cataracts foam 'stead of smooth-flowing fountains
I sigh for the valley of dark Lochnagar.

**Lord Byron**

On the Spittal of Glenshee,
Which is most dismal for to see,
With its bleak and rugged mountains,
And clear, crystal, spouting fountains
With their misty foam;
And thousands of sheep there together doth roam,
Browsing on the barren pasture most gloomy to see.
Stunted in heather, and scarcely a tree,
Which is enough to make the traveller weep,
The loneliness thereof and the bleating of the sheep.

**Sir William Topaz McGonagall**

The idea of life imitating art is central to my interpretation of McGonagall's experiences. The observant reader with a modest knowledge of Western art will recognize borrowings from a number of well-known images to illustrate episodes from his life and poetry. It is by no means the only strategy I have used, but McGonagall loved to be thought of alongside the great and the good, and pictorial parodies were destined to play a central role. I am not going to identify them all here, as the experience of personally interpreting the illustrations is a vital component of enjoying them. Those seeking clues as to the origin of these parodies need only look at some of the names of artists who appear in the acknowledgements section.

Another important question that lay behind my creation of this work was: could I express in visual terms why we find him so funny? Well, vanity and the inability to accept our insignificance in the general scheme of things is a form of megalomania that has driven dictators to commit mass murder – which is not very funny. But, in McGonagall's case his megalomania was harmless. He just wanted to be a world-famous poet. Many more talented men and women have conspicuously failed to achieve his level of notoriety, and so we find it comforting to laugh at him.

I would not be the first to observe that he makes us feel good about our modest abilities because his were so monumentally bad. Yet there is something strangely compelling about his story.

You simply cannot separate his prolific output of doggerel from his posturing as a great poet. **Knowing** the way he conducted his life makes his verse hilarious rather than just bad. Illustrating his life and verse together has been my way of expressing this. For no matter how many times he was rebuffed and ridiculed, he pursued his Muse with relentless zeal and unwavering self-belief. Many other artists have been persecuted in the same way, but, later, posterity has conferred on them the status of genius.

Why should McGonagall not have hoped for the same recognition? Burdened with this thought, his heroism can seem both tragic and comical at the same time. He reminds us that ambition is no defence against mortality, whether we are successful in life or not. When we laugh at his pretensions and misfortunes we are really laughing at our own. His life has certainly afforded more than one generation entertainment and cause for reflection. Hopefully, it will continue to do so for generations to come. It is the least he would have wanted!

Above all else, this work is a personal interpretation of a legend. Readers will be pleased to know that there is now a memorial plaque in Edinburgh's Greyfriars Cemetery to the great man's memory, but there wasn't when I made the drawing of his burial that appears in this book. Evidence, perhaps, that there is a growing body of opinion that believes it is perfectly possible to laugh at McGonagall's verse and still respect the legendary life of the man who created it.

My contribution to McGonagall's 'Immortal Memory' (or should I say 'Immoral Mammary'?) is to try and turn his legend into a work of art.

Charles Nasmyth

*'Failure is unimportant. It takes courage to make a fool of yourself.'*

*Charlie Chaplin*

# The Moon

Beautiful Moon, with thy silvery light,
Thou seemest most charming to my sight;
As I gaze upon thee in the sky so high
A tear of joy does moisten mine eye.

Beautiful Moon, with thy silvery light,
Thou cheerest the Esquimau in the night;
For thou lettest him see to harpoon the fish,
And with them he makes a dainty dish.

Beautiful Moon, with thy silvery light,
Thou cheerest the fox in the night,
And lettest him see to steal the grey goose away
Out of the farm-yard from a stack of hay.

Beautiful Moon, with thy silvery light,
Thou cheerest the farmer in the night,
And makest his heart beat with delight
As he views his crops by the light in the night.

Beautiful Moon, with thy silvery light,
Thou cheerest the eagle in the night,
And lettest him see to devour his prey
And carry it to his nest away.

Beautiful Moon, with thy silvery light,
Thou cheerest the mariner in the
night As he paces the deck alone, Thinking of his dear
friends at home.

Beautiful Moon, with thy silvery light,
Thou cheerest the weary traveller in the night;
For thou lightest up the wayside around
To him when he is homeward bound.

Beautiful Moon, with thy silvery light,
Thou cheerest the lovers in the night
As they walk through the shady groves along,
Making love to each other before they go home.

Beautiful Moon, with thy silvery light, Thou cheerest
the poacher in the night; For thou lettest him see to set his snares To catch the rabbits
and the hares.

After leaving Orkney, the McGonagalls moved to the bonnie City of Dundee.

Royal Arch, Dundee.

In Queen Victoria's day 'twas famous for its jute mills and whaling ships.

Young William was apprenticed as a hand loom weaver in Scouringburn.

After mastering the handloom, he started reading a lot of Shakespeare at night.

Once, McGonagall was wholly familiar with the characters of Macbeth, Richard III, Hamlet and Othello, he would enact scenes from the plays to entertain his shopmates.

Spurred by his success as a thespian at the mill in Scouringburn, McGonagall offered his services to Mr Giles' Penny Theatre in Lindsay Street. He was invited to play the part of Macbeth, provided he paid Mr Giles one pound in cash, before the performance. His workmates, keen to promote his career outside weaving, made a collection to pay his subscription. It was money well spent, because McGonagall's interpretation of the role was rich with idiosyncrasies.

Although McGonagall considered himself to be one of the greatest Shakespearian actors in the world, posterity has remembered him for another talent.

Listen, McGonagall, you ✶✶✶✶✶✶ idiot! You're supposed to die in this scene!

At the end of the play Macbeth is supposed to die in mortal combat with Macduff. In McGonagall's debut in the leading role he decided that Macduff's struggle for victory should not be easy, and he knocked the other actor to the floor repeatedly until his annoyance and fatigue became apparent to the audience, who found it very entertaining. However, despite this early success, it was poetry that became his true forte....

'The most startling incident of my life, was the time I discovered myself to be a poet, which was in the year of 1877'. The bard sat alone in his room during the Dundee holiday week, depressed because he couldn't get to the Highlands 'to see the beautiful scenery', when The Muse visited him and whispered in his ear.....

Write! Write!

'I know nothing about poetry' he thought, but 'a flame, as Lord Byron has said, seemed to kindle up my entire frame, along with a desire to write poetry'. In no time he had penned a verse in memory of Rev' George Gilfillan.

# An Address to the Reverend George Gilfillan.

Rev. George Gilfillan of Dundee,
There is none can you excel;
You have boldly rejected the Confession of Faith
And defended your cause right well.

The first time I heard him speak,
'Twas in the Kinnaird Hall,
Lecturing on the Garibaldi movement,
As loud as he could bawl.

He is a liberal gentleman
To the poor while in distress,
And for his kindness unto them
The Lord will surely bless.

My blessing on his noble form,
And on his lofty head,
May all good angels guard him while living
And hereafter when he's dead.

The Reverend George Gilfillan was a legendary Dundee preacher, and McGonagall considered the man to be his friend. Indeed, Gilfillan had once written him a testimonial when seeking employment as an actor. So, in his new calling as a poet, McGonagall dedicated his first poem, 'composed while under divine inspiration', to the worthy minister.

In a little over two years from his first visitation by The Muse, McGonagall had found the inspiration for his tragic masterwork 'The Tay Bridge Disaster'. The bridge, designed by Thomas Bouch, fell down eighteen months after being opened.

Queen Victoria travelled over the bridge in August 1879, and was so impressed by Bouch's enormous erection that she had him knighted at Windsor Castle.

The Tay Bridge not long after it was completed and shortly before it fell down.

My, my, Sir Thomas, when I said, 'arise' I never expected anything like that!

Nothing to worry about Ma'am, just a rivet for the Tay Bridge .....always carry a spare in my pocket.

Workmen constructing the iron columns that supported the first Tay Bridge.

The huge span of iron and steel was fully two miles in length, but the 500 construction workers who helped Bouch get it up, some of whom lost their lives in the process, were not honoured with knighthoods. Ominously, not long after the bridge was opened, rivets were found to be loose and cracks were appearing.

The cracks were painted over with a substance called 'Beaumont's Egg', a mixture of iron filings & beeswax.

In the kitchens of Dundee, a similar concoction was created to celebrate the opening of the faulty structure. It was called 'Tay Bridge Sauce.'

What's on the menu today, my good woman?

Tatties and 'Tay Bridge Sauce', Mr McGonagall.

TAY BRIDGE SAUCE

Ulysses Grant at Vicksburg 1863.

Unaware of its parlous condition, many foreign dignitaries visited the bridge during the last stages of its construction. They included an American gentleman called Ulysses S. Grant, who was reputed to have a drink problem, but it did not prevent him from helping the North to defeat the Confederacy in the American Civil War and, later, becoming President of the United States. It is likely that his visit to the Tay Bridge in 1877 was made during a tour of the distilleries.

The prestige that the Tay Bridge project attracted to Scotland and the British Empire was short lived. The central section collapsed in a storm on the 28th December 1879, taking with it a train and all its passengers. An event..........

...'Which will be remember'd for a very long time.'
Wm McGonagall 'The Tay Bridge Disaster.'

Bouch was held responsible for the disaster and died a broken man the following year. He was buried in Dean Cemetery, Edinburgh, where his grave is marked by a magnificent tombstone and overhung by a holly tree. This is periodically cut back to prevent the leaves from obscuring the engineer's finely sculpted portrait.

If McGonagall had been familiar with this peaceful Victorian burial place, he might well have written a poetic eulogy about some of the famous corpses that lie beneath its soil.

He was, after all, the poet who bewailed the passing of two Scottish aristocrats with the immortal words:

'Alas Lord & Lady Dalhousie are dead, and buried at last, Which causes many people to feel a little downcast.....'

The Evening Telegraph

APPALLING
DISASTER
IN DUNDEE

TAY BRIDGE WRECKED

TRAIN THROWN INTO
THE RIVER

However, McGonagall could only occasionally afford the luxury of travelling to interesting places for poetic inspiration. More often than not he would peruse the daily papers to ignite his creative passion. Even when the tragedian lived near to a disaster site, he chose to extract most of the information for his epic masterpiece 'The Tay Bridge Disaster' from a newspaper.

# The Tay Bridge Disaster.

Beautiful Railway Bridge of the Silvery Tay!
Alas! I am very sorry to say
That ninety lives have been taken away
On the last Sabbath day of 1879
Which will be remember'd for a very long time.

'Twas about seven o'clock at night,
And the wind it blew with all its might,
And the rain came pouring down,
And the dark clouds seemed to frown,
And the Demon of the air seemed to say—
"I'll blow down the Bridge of Tay."

When the train left Edinburgh
The passengers hearts were light and felt no sorrow,
But Boreas blew a terrific gale
Which made their hearts for to quail,
And many of the passengers with fear did say—
"I hope God will send us safe across the Bridge of Tay."

But when the train came near to Wormit Bay
Boreas he did loud and angry bray,
And shook the central girders of the Bridge of Tay
On the last Sabbath day of 1879,
Which will be remember'd for a very long time.

So the train sped on with all its might,
And Bonnie Dundee soon have in sight,
And the passengers' hearts felt light,
Thinking they would enjoy themselves on the New Year,
With their friends at home they lov'd most dear,
And wish them all a happy New Year.

So the train mov'd slowly along the Bridge of Tay,
Until it was about midway,
Then the central girders with a crash gave way,
And down went the train and passengers into the Tay!
The Storm Fiend did loudly bray,
Because ninety lives had been taken away,
On the last Sabbath day of 1879,
Which will be remember'd for a very long time.

It must have been an awful sight,
To witness in the dusky moonlight,
While the storm fiend did laugh, and angry did bray,
Along the Railway Bridge of the Silv'ry Tay.
Oh! ill-fated Bridge of the Silv'ry Tay......

......I must now conclude my lay
By telling the world fearlessly without the least dismay,
That your central girders would not have given way,
At least many sensible men do say,
Had they been supported on each side with buttresses,
At least many sensible men confesses,
For the stronger we our houses do build,
The less chance we have of being killed.

Although McGonagall confessed a profound affection for Dundee, which was expressed in his many poems devoted to its triumphs and disasters, the city only rewarded him with a life of poverty and the cruel contempt of its more uncouth citizens; particularly the publicans. The bard frequently recited his poems in pubs for a small fee to make up the money he had lost through giving up his job as a weaver.

He believed that publicans tried to stop him from plying his trade, because it distracted the customers from buying more drink. Sometimes, they would throw wet towels in his face to belittle him.

On other occasions they would hide the poet's stick in the hope that it would deter him from visiting again.

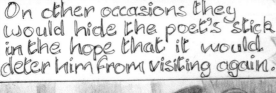

A close up of a dried pea, which can hurt if thrown hard.

Some publicans even took to pelting him with dried peas in an attempt to silence him, but it only served to fuel his moral and excessive fervour!

For many years Dundee only remembered McGonagall with a small square of modern housing situated between Step Row and Paton's Lane, where the bard had lodgings during his time in the city. The statue of Queen Victoria is much grander.

McGONAGALL SQUARE

Determined to spread his reputation beyond the boundaries of a city that didn't really appreciate him, William, armed with his very own business card, set out on a series of travels to bring his verse to a wider public. His wife, Jean, whom he rarely mentions, was forced to work in the laundry of an asylum to make ends meet.

Wm. McGonagall
L.J.A.R.
(Lyric Inditer and Reciter)
Successor to Wm. Shakespeare
Poetry Promptly Executed

Like many other Dundonians, the bard venerated the British monarch. Convinced that the lady who made Lord Tennyson her Poet Laureate would also grant him an audience, he set out on his epic journey from Dundee to the royal residence at Balmoral. A return walk of 120 miles.

At the time of writing, 100 years after the poet's death, Dundee intends to raise a statue to him costing about £30,000.

It was a fine day of sunshine when the poet left Dundee to present his poems to the Queen at Balmoral.

The walk there took him three days and two nights. The first night was spent in Alyth.

DUNDEE
20 MILES ←
ALYTH
SPITTAL
OF
GLENSHEE
20 MILES →

William prevailed on the charity of shepherds for shelter at night who provided him with humble fare and a place to sleep.

He falls asleep in the arms of Morpheus.

On the second night he slept in a barn. At first, the rugged scenery around Glen Shee and the exciting prospect of a meeting with the Queen prevented him from sleeping. Eventually, he fell asleep in the arms of Morpheus & was affected by ......

....strange dreams that found him wandering alone through misty mountains in pursuit of his Holy Grail. An apparition of Her Majesty coming to meet him in a carriage and four evaporated to be replaced by an extremely aggressive Newfoundland dog that attacks him in front of Balmoral.

The poet's dream is an ill omen.

On the Spittal of Glenshee
Which is most dismal for to
see,
With its bleak and rugged
mountains,
And clear, crystal, spouting fountains
With their misty foam,
And thousands of sheep there doth
roam,

Browsing on the barren
pasture most gloomy to see.
Stunted in heather, and
scarcely a tree.
Which is enough to make the
traveller weep,
The loneliness thereof and the
bleating of the sheep.

A Medley of British
Imperial War Verse

Success to Tommy Atkins, he's a very brave man,
And to deny it there's few people can;
And to face his foreign foes he's never afraid,
Therefore he's not a beggar, as Rudyard Kipling has said.

Oh, think of Tommy Atkins when from home far away,
Lying on the battlefield, earth's cold clay;
And a stone or his knapsack pillowing his head,
And his comrades lying near by him wounded and dead.

And in conclusion I will say,
Don't forget his wife and children when he's far away;
But try and help them all you can,
For remember Tommy Atkins is a very useful man.

Ye sons of Great Britain, I think no shame
To write in praise of brave General Graham!
Whose name will be handed down to posterity without any stigma,
Because, at the battle of El-Teb, he defeated Osman Digna.

By two o'clock they were fairly beat
And Osman Digna, the false prophet, was forced to retreat
After three hours' of an incessant fight;
But Heaven, 'tis said, defends the right.

And I think he ought to be ashamed of himself,
For I consider he has acted the part of a silly elf,
By thinking to conquer the armies of the Lord
With his foolish and benighted rebel horde.

Verses selected
from the poems
'Lines in Praise
of Tommy Atkins'
&
'The Battle of
El-Teb,'
by William McGonagall.

Undeterred by his rejection at the gates of Balmoral, William's odyssey in pursuit of fame continued with increased determination. One autumn, he travelled to Kinross and Fife in the hope of finding venues where he could recite his poems to enraptured audiences. Unfortunately, his attempt to use the Temperance Hall in Kinross failed.

Magnificent Poem on Loch Leven
Beautiful Loch Leven, near by Kinross
For a good day's fishing the angler is seldom at a loss,
For the loch it abounds with pike and trout,
Which can be had for the catching without any doubt,
And the scenery around is most beautiful to be seen, Especially the castle wherein was imprisoned Scotland's ill-starred Queen.

Notwithstanding his disappointment in Kinross, he was inspired to write some wonderful verse on the glories of Loch Leven. However, the coal mining villages of Cowdenbeath and Lochgelly also failed to provide an audience, and the ancient burgh of Dunfermline turned its back on him altogether. One gentleman of Fife even had the temerity to suggest his poems were dreadful. So he returned home destitute.

Your poetry is truly awful.

William's next trip was to the great City of London. There he hoped to secure some engagements in music halls. The money for this trip – five pounds – was supplied by the Irish dramatist, Boucicault, who took pity on the impecunious Dundonian when he learned some practical jokers had tricked the bard into believing he had arranged to meet him in an expensive restaurant. The trip was not a great success as McGonagall failed to gain any bookings in theatreland. Nevertheless, like the poet, Wordsworth, in 'The Prelude', William found inspiration in the city's crowded streets and fine buildings.

The kindly D. Boucicault
1820 – 1890

The Houses of Parliament.

Whilst in London, the poet attempted to visit Sir Henry Irving, the great actor. Although William considered himself to be Irving's equal, his opinion was not shared by the porter.

The Lyceum
Presents
SIR HENRY IRVING

AS MACBETH

Sir 'Enry dahn't wanna see the likes of you in 'ere.

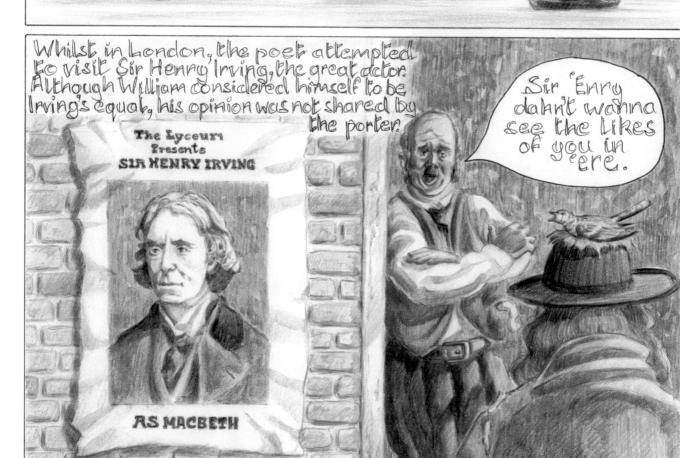

O Friend! one feeling was there which belonged
To this great city, by exclusive right;
How often in the overflowing streets,
Have I gone forwards with the crowd, and said
Unto myself, 'The face of every one
That passes by me is a mystery!'
Thus have I looked, nor ceased to look, oppressed
By thoughts of what and wither, when and how,
Until the shapes before my eyes became
A second-sight procession, such as glides
Over still mountains, or appears in dreams....
   Wm. Wordsworth            'The Prelude'

As I stood upon London Bridge,
And viewed the mighty throng
Of thousands of people in cabs and buses
Rapidly whirling along,
And driving to and fro,
Up one street and down another
As quick as they could go.

Then I was struck with the discordant sounds
Of human voices there,
Which seemed to me like wild geese
      Cackling in the air.
   Wm McGonagall           'Jottings of London'

ELEPHANT
AND
CASTLE

So William found nowhere to perform his work and sold none of his poems. Eventually, he had to write to Mr Alexander C. Lamb, a friend and proprietor of the Temperance Hotel in Dundee, for the money to get home. New York, which he compared to Babylon, left a lasting impression.

William, on his return from New York was never to travel as far again. He left Dundee and went to live in Perth. During his residence in the 'Fair City' he was sent yet another hoax letter. This time it was signed by one C. Macdonald 'Poet Laureate of Burmah' and awarded our poet the title 'Topaz McGonagall, Knight of the White Elephant of Burmah'. The award was made, allegedly, on behalf of 'King Theebaw of Burmah and the Andaman Islands.

The Sheriff Court in the City of Perth.

Court of King Theebaw
Andaman Islands
Dec. 2, 1894.

Dear and Most Highly Honoured Sir;
I have been requested to inform you that you were lately appointed a Grand Knight of the Holy Order of the White Elephant, Burmah.
By Order of His Royal Highness the King
Topaz General, Topaz Minister Secretary of State, Holder of Seals. Registrar-General, Staff-Bearer. Secretary of Letters Patent. Keeper of the White Elephant.

The insignia of the knighthood was a silver elephant attached to a green silk ribbon.

The bard was more than happy to adopt his newly awarded title but found Perth a little too small to make a living in, even though he thought the inhabitants to be friendly souls. So, in pursuit of further recognition, he made a number of forays onto the stage in Glasgow to recite his own poems and popular extracts from the works of Shakespeare.

William Power, a journalist, recalls that during one of McGonagall's performances in the Albion Halls, he was pelted with all manner of rotten fruit, vegetables and eggs. The poet's response was to shout his verse even louder, whilst slashing at the missiles with his sword. He was treated in much the same way in Edinburgh where he spent his final years.

41

As an old man, the poet claimed to like Edinburgh but was treated with no respect by students who would hold dinners in his honour and throw food at him. It was here that he finally died on the same day as Emile Zola, the 29th September 1902

Emile Zola after Monet.

McGonagall after tea.

Sir William Topaz McGonagall, Knight of the White Elephant of Burmah, was buried in the cemetery of Greyfriars Kirk, Edinburgh, the final resting place of many eminent Scots, including the poets, Duncan Ban McIntyre and Allan Ramsay. Even a dog called 'Bobby' has a memorial, but the grave of McGonagall remains unmarked.

Had the impoverished bard been able to afford a headstone, a fitting epitaph might have been from his beloved Shakespeare.

'Life's but a walking shadow; a poor player

That struts and frets his hour upon the stage,

Macbeth
Act V, Scene V.

And then is heard no more: it is a tale Told by an idiot, full of sound and fury, Signifying nothing.'

# The McGonagall Supper

Anyone who tried to lay down strict guidelines on how to run a McGonagall Supper would be missing the point. It constitutes an evening where anarchy and the imagination should be given free rein. It was first-hand experience of this that led to the creation of this book, and it is about some of those experiences that I now write.

Being English, I have learnt much about the alternative perspective on the universe in my adopted home of Scotland, but I naturally assumed it wouldn't have much to teach me about eccentric and exhibitionist behaviour. The English have always been considered pre-eminent in such virtues by the rest of the world, but I was soon to discover that they did not have an outright monopoly. Even more surprising, it was that bastion of Edinburgh's bourgeoisie, the Round Table of Corstorphine, which was directly responsible for my enlightenment. Once a year, this worthy association of businessmen and professionals would drop their respectable guard, and organize a McGonagall Supper to raise money for charities such as the Children's Hospice Association of Scotland. Money was raised by charging for the ticket a price that far exceeded the cost of the 'meal'. Curiously enough, well over a hundred guests were sometimes happy to part with their money in this way, and I was soon to find out why.

The first thing a novice attending one of these events has to learn is that dress is always formal. For gentlemen, this often consists of: a cap, scarf, old jacket, **nicky tams** (trousers tied up around the calves with string) and a pair of old boots. A collarless shirt is good underneath the jacket, but the important thing is to look shabby.

For ladies, a ceremonial rolling pin replaces the usual evening bag.

Stockings should always be worn wrinkled or laddered.

'Rags' lend an appropriate air of incorrectness to the evening, but use the theatrical type to avoid arrest by the health police.

Nicky tams are a sartorial 'must' for gentlemen.

'Dress is always formal.'

I have never attended a McGonagall Supper at which ladies were present, but there is absolutely no reason at all why they shouldn't be. At a mixed event, their dress code might be something like a female equivalent of the above: headscarf, with hair in rollers, dirty blouse, ragged skirt and hefty pair of shoes. An old-fashioned floral housecoat with a pair of laddered stockings might be good, but the important thing to remember is that you are free to improvise.

Broadly speaking, the format of a McGonagall Supper is the reverse of a Burns Supper. Whereas a Burns Supper traditionally starts with a welcome from the Chairman, a McGonagall Supper starts with a farewell from the Heidyin (literally 'the head one'). The programme of events at the latter then works its way back to the Heidyin's welcome at the end of the evening. The meal, often starting with cheese and biscuits, finishes with the soup. The idea of reversal is also extended to the way the tables are set for the meal, with all the cutlery laid upside down on sheets of newspaper instead of a tablecloth.

It will come as no surprise that the food itself is kept cheap and simple, which, if you are running one of these events for charity, will maximize your takings. The main course of the evening, replacing the traditional haggis of a Burns Night, is stovies. Sometimes known in the programme as 'Mighty McGonagall Mash', this delicious mush of leftover meat, potatoes and grease, at the suppers I attended, was 'piped' into the room by everyone playing the theme from *The Dam Busters* on a comb and piece of toilet paper. The 'Address to the Haggis' was then replaced by the 'Address to the Stovies'. This is one of the many opportunities that the evening provides for some free improvisation, of which I here give a brief example:

Mighty McGonagall Mash

**To a Haggis**
Fair fa' your honest, sonsie face
Great Chieftain o' the Puddin-race!
Aboon them a' ye tak your place,
Painch, tripe, or thairm:
Weel are ye wordy o' a grace
As lang's my arm.

**To the Stovies**
A pile of tatties in your place
Such fitting fare to stuff your face!
With plenty o' sauce you must lace,
Pour'd all o'er guid and thick,
To stop yer feeling slightly sick.

As commonly occurs at Burns Night, there is usually a 'Loyal Toast' at some point in the evening where I have heard of guests actually being served toast. However, more commonly it appeared as an item in the paper programme of the events I attended as 'Toast – available all night'. What I have never heard of happening but would seem most appropriate, bearing in mind McGonagall's lifelong infatuation with her, would be a toast to Queen Victoria!

Much more important though, are the toasts that are made at regular intervals to the bard. These are usually heralded by the Heidyin, or anyone who can shout loud enough, calling out 'McGonagall!' On hearing this, all the assembled arise and raise their glasses to intone the traditional toast:

**William Topaz McGonagall –**
**May his name be remembered for a very, very, long time!**

On one occasion, I estimated that this happened about twenty times during the course of the meal.

After the stovies and the soup have been consumed, it is usually time for the 'Immoral Mammary'. Like the 'Immortal Memory' at a Burns Supper, this can be a tribute to Scotland's alternative bard in words and verse. However, the attention span of the audience for this event always seems somewhat reduced when compared to the Burns Night equivalent. More often than not, it ends up with the speaker being pelted with bread rolls and any other leftover food that happens to be lying around. It is, perhaps, a tradition that recalls the days when McGonagall was bombarded with food every time he attempted to entertain an audience.

Once the 'Immoral Mammary' has taken over from the 'Immortal Memory', 'The Tay Bridge Disaster' takes over from 'Tam o' Shanter'.

Having been involved in the recitation of 'The Tay Bridge Disaster' from my first McGonagall Supper, I still regard it as the high point of the evening. How this great masterpiece of doggerel is interpreted is entirely up to the imagination of the performers. Usually, one person declaims the verse as loudly as possible whilst the other performers use a variety of props to interpret each section of the poem. As I explained in my opening notes, I used a variety of cardboard cut-outs to do this, and some of the imagery found its way into the illustrations for this book. Lines such as: 'Which made their hearts for to quail' were quite literally interpreted as hearts turning into quails. The point in the poem where the train crashes into the Tay was sometimes dramatized by dropping a toy train into a bucket, and at the line 'It must have been an awful sight to witness in the pale moonlight', a cardboard cut-out of the moon was raised above one of the performers seated on a toilet bowl boiling over with dry ice. Then, near the end of the poem, when McGonagall declares 'I must now conclude my lay', an inflatable sex toy was passed over the top of a screen and wrestled to the floor in a frenzy of erotic passion by another performer. There was, of course, much more besides this, and it always varied from year to year as the deep well of the puerile imagination can never be fully exhausted.

After this, the remaining part of the evening was devoted to community singing with folk bands and further toasts to the bard. Other traditions, that I have so far left unmentioned, went on throughout the night. One of the most memorable of these was the passing round of a huge glass Wellington boot filled with several litres of beer. Once someone had drained the

A huge glass welly filled with beer.

boot of ale, it was passed back to the previous drinker who had the unenviable task of paying for the re-fill. As a charity event, the Heidyin would periodically declare that all drinking must be done with the left hand, whilst a Sergeant-at-Arms would wander round with a bucket to collect fines from those caught drinking with their right. Hundreds of pounds were often raised in this manner.

All organizers of McGonagall Nights have their own traditions. I have heard that at some events a stripper walks into the room stark naked and proceeds to put all her clothes back on in front of the guests. Quite outrageous and it goes without saying I have never been present on such an occasion. At Corstorphine's McGonagall Suppers, I am happy to say that a real sense of decorum was always maintained. Every year, without fail, the evening would finish very formally with the same song and dance routine. All the assembled would climb onto the tables and drop their trousers, whilst waving their hands in the air and giving full voice to 'Singing in the Rain'. There were never any women present at these particular events, but, had there been so, I am sure they would have made an equally imaginative decision as to which item of clothing to discard. Which is a very good reason for making sure the McGonagall Night Supper never becomes a final redoubt of male chauvinism.

I'm singing in the rain